THE CROSSED-OUT SWASTIKA

The Crossed-Out Swastika

Cyrus Cassells

Copper Canyon Press
Port Townsend, Washington

Cover art: Eamon O'Kane, *Track 3*

Copper Canyon Press is in residence at Fort Worden
State Park in Port Townsend, Washington, under the
auspices of Centrum. Centrum is a gathering place for
artists and creative thinkers from around the world,
students of all ages and backgrounds, and audiences
seeking extraordinary cultural enrichment.

LIBRARY OF CONGRESS
CATALOGING-IN-PUBLICATION DATA

Cassells, Cyrus.
The crossed-out swastika / Cyrus Cassells.
    p. cm.
ISBN 978-1-55659-379-6 (pbk.)
1. World War, 1939–1945 — Poetry. I. Title.
PS3553.A7955C76 2012
811'.54 — dc23

                                        2011043022

Copper Canyon Press
Post Office Box 271
Port Townsend, Washington 98368

www.coppercanyonpress.org

In memory of Pierre Seel
1923–2005

ACKNOWLEDGMENTS

My gratitude to the National Endowment for the Arts, the Rockefeller Foundation, the Fine Arts Work Center in Provincetown, the Lannan Foundation, and Badger-dog Press for residencies that made possible the writing of this book, and to Texas State University-San Marcos for providing me with developmental leave.

Heartfelt thanks to Peter Adamov, Margo Berdeshevsky, Greg Blaine, Toi Derricotte, Martín Espada, Charles Adès Fishman, Carolyn Forché, Suzanne Gardinier, Jeremy Halinen, Ellen Hinsey, Achim Kramer, Erika Kramer, Li-Young Lee, Harry Mattison, Daniel Mendelsohn, William Merwin, Anne Michaels, Eamon O'Kane, Alicia Ostriker, Judith Pacht, Nicholas Samaras, Robert Stanley, Jean Valentine, and Adam Zagajewski.

Poems in *The Crossed-Out Swastika,* some in earlier versions, appeared in the following anthologies and journals: *Against Agamemnon: War Poetry 2009* (Waterwood Press), *Blood to Remember: American Poets on the Holocaust* (Time Being Books), *Borderlands, The Broadkill Review, Cadence of Hooves: A Celebration of Horses* (Yarroway Mountain Press), *Cimarron Review, Knockout Literary Magazine, New Works Review, Prism: An Interdisciplinary Journal for Holocaust Educators, Shirim,* and *The Weight of Addition: An Anthology of Texas Poetry* (Mutabilis Press).

Birds you killed, fish you tossed into your boat,
In what words will they find rest and in what Heaven?

— CZESLAW MILOSZ
THE SEPARATE NOTEBOOKS

CONTENTS

Pencil and Dragon-Slayer   3
Elegy with an Owl in It   9
Riders on the Back of Silence   10
The Singing Forest   23
Sabine Who Was Hidden in the Mountains   26
The Fit   33

⁝

My Secret Throne   49
The Galician Spade   52
The Ravine   53
Three Kings   54
Salute   55
The Young Doctor from Krakow   57
Primo Levi Remembering Dante in Auschwitz   64
Juliek's Violin   67
A Great Beauty   69

⁝

The Postcard of Sophie Scholl   73
The Confiscated Shoes   76
Auschwitz, All Hallows   77

Notes   81
About the Author   83

THE CROSSED-OUT SWASTIKA

PENCIL AND DRAGON-SLAYER

1. Resurrected Pages

In night terrors, the war's a raging hunter
shouldering a brace of birds;

in night terrors, when I open my mouth,
everything's mute, confiscated —

as suddenly a hand in a snowbank
I spotted as a boy

(while wielding a pretend baton,
while aping a local maestro)

surges out of the ruins
of my shelled precinct —

If I risk the pages
tucked in a mustard tin

cached long ago,
I know I'll resurrect

fish sellers bereft of fish,
bakers orphaned of flour,

the city still pinioned, eviscerated —
Listed in an aged yet legible entry

are a knockabout boy's pure trophies
pilfered from a shattered tailor shop:

a not-rusted penknife
and a pine-green spool of thread,

precious to my thrifty mother,
a windfall jacket

and a woolen scarf that I dubbed
my lucky armor...

Adept at hide-and-seek,
a rubble rat in a blistered district,

listen, I had a childhood
of dead-sure cowboys

and dream buffalo,
of faux fishing poles

and make-believe marbles,
in those years that can't be tallied

like other years,
when it was illegal

to touch a camera,
so scribbled words became

equivalent to snapshots,
an empty-bellied boy's respite

in a cloud-blackened Europe
of brutal roll calls,

quickly buried letters,
bricked-up gold.

II. **There Are No Children Here**

Adolf, the upending dreamer,
he was a rebuffed painter,

let me remind you.
And when his acolytes insisted,

alluding to their burr-like camps,
es gibt hier keine Kinder

(there are no children here),
in one sense

it was unalloyed truth:
a kid cast off, I was relegated to

the shadow of their vision of heaven:
and no Valhalla-bound heart,

no dream-laden easel,
no lofty fanatic ever admits

ensuing cries of failed infants —
the first act of the play the last:

the first gazebo,
the first garden lamp,

the first busy nest glimpsed
in the earliest park,

and no words to pin them yet,
no handles for this fleeting vision:

baled hay, waving hands, bits of blue
spied from a chink in a boxcar,

a wick-thin boy, baring his numbered flesh, become
the shadow of their vision of heaven—

III. Pencil and Dragon-Slayer

Hear me: my boyhood was a suitcase
ready by the door,

a bomb-cratered bridge,
a punishing nightscape. If I declared

When I was a child, I had no childhood
(as Chekhov once lamented),

well, it wouldn't be entirely true:
beyond my imperiled father's desperate

briberies and forgeries,
there were moments

when a blasted maple branch
was magic,

when my filched coat seemed
benevolent as a beekeeper's veil,

inviolate against the fierce swarm
of the first weeks of occupation;

mornings when I imagined
a clear-eyed boy with hoarded paper

and a scavenged pencil
might prevail, in secret,

as an invincible dragon-slayer
and live to become

a whistling but able street sweeper,
a matinee gangster or buccaneer,

someday when the fanged and fiery world
became the world again.

ELEGY WITH AN OWL IN IT

The young, the war-buffeted, the banished —
they were blossom-and-fruit-seeking

branch lovers,
braid-in-the-inkwell schemers,

and their time under watchtowers,
brief as relinquished myrrh,

brisk as an owlet fluttering against
a soldier's insignia.

RIDERS ON THE BACK OF SILENCE

Brooklyn, the present day

I. The Spirit Box

Son:

A son is a steadfast
keeper of secrets,

a cupped palm, a calyx,
a son is a spirit box, listen —

I was born after armistice,
the fissured cities,

but slept nights
with a human smoke.

And though I never shuddered
from a black rouge

of rationed coffee
to keep clean,

the frost and sullen mud
of a forced march,

the unspoken, the unspeakable,
became my life:

I was a boy bathed in dreams
by a menorah fashioned against

the penalty of death,
a mysterious klezmer.

A son is a spirit box, imagine.

II. **Riders on the Back of Silence**

Son:

As a boy, my old-world aunts and uncles
would weep when I entered the room:

What did I have to do with sadness?
Their cryptic tears

and purse-tucked Kleenex
were my own tantalizing

Hardy Boys case to crack.
Gradually, as a junior detective, I grasped

how much I resembled
an uncle lost in the war,

and like the savvy, querying boy
at the Passover Seder

become a scrupulous man,
an inquisitive reporter,

I set out to track my look-alike's,
my family's wartime destiny—

What my father marshaled against,
what my mother endured,

the unspoken, the unspeakable,
became my mission:

though I was born in a venomless
time and suburb,

phantoms, chimeras breathed
in our never-quite-here-and-now house,

secret calendars of fire:
Mother, I dreamed we were

riders on the back of silence,
the wild unsaid beneath us:

horse, whale,
behemoth.

We never spoke of the war.
So with stark reading,

a well-thumbed
Diary of Anne Frank,

I resolved to imagine
pitiless showers,

whips and watchtowers
of brute commanders,

their Gypsy-less, Jew-less,
jerry-rigged heaven.

III. **The Photojournalist**

Son:

In my search for your cloud-wrapped past,
Mother,

the wounded earth became mine,
and each time I aligned myself

with the exiled, the dispossessed,
I aligned myself with you.

Apprenticed to, obsessed with,
light and justice,

always I've tried to bring into focus
a girl, with war as her spur,

with hunger as her horse
and shadow —

Mother, in El Salvador
I couldn't lift my camera

to capture the unearthed
bodies of silenced nuns:

I'm almost, but never quite,
inured to death:

a child in a jacket of flies;
the last typed lines of a friend,

a dissident poet whose body
was opened beyond belief—

In the Secret Annex, in the countless
precincts of strife, I've learned

an Esperanto of blood and hope
and forbearance,

as if someday I might receive my wish:
to read, on a night as serene as truce,

your long-awaited story:
the capo's unrelenting curses,

a castaway's pain:
I should know it by heart, Mother.

iv. **The Antimiracle**

Mother:

At the spring's start, there were fists
rather than fragrance,

April-upon-April hope
braided with arrests and betrayals,

as dark as the derided
spaces in our censored mail.

Garrisons, watchtowers,
checkpoints as daunting as Gorgons,

proliferated.
The borders became too-tight belts—

Long after the white of truce,
in restless sleep I struggled

to awaken the family dead,
to confess, unabashed:

Lampshades of sullied flesh,
linens fashioned of human hair—

I was not prepared
to stand outside humanity—

v. **The Pet Name**

Son:

Soft as a fontanel,
Dove was the pet name

you gave me as a boy,
and on the world's battlefields,

like a drop of holy water,
its bolstering sweetness

became my talisman.
It was with me, mitigating, winged,

shielding me somehow,
as my lover Jaeger's lens shattered

and his lifeblood
soaked into my shirt.

It was with me,
a thousand leagues from God,

when I photographed
a gassed village —

whole families
and their livestock hushed

as if by an invisible hand,
as if some heedless, insane baker

had dusted the afternoon
with flour.

VI. **Trains**

Mother:

Today, amid the earliest birdcalls, the first
neighborhood sounds,

I swept the stoop,
leaned on the trusty broom,

and wondered:
If I could write, son, about those years,

where would I begin? —
Your grandfather was a stationmaster,

tall as a flagpole
and as taciturn.

And though his owl-gray eyes
have gone to earth,

I keep thinking he'll round the corner
in his fastidious clothes,

carrying a sprig of asphodel
or fragrant honeysuckle —

so dignified with his gold
spectacles and timetables.

God took him the Sabbath before
the shouts and stones, the smashed

storefronts of *Kristallnacht.*
How it would've angered him to see

that his beloved trains
were used to betray us.

VII. Dove's Arc

Mother:

For years I dreamed maternal dreams
of your cozy security —

spacious freedom from pogroms,
all the misery the wide,

unmerciful world doles out
to Jews and scapegoats,

and always you seemed
determined to court danger —

So you want to know
about a prisoner's,

a *Häftling*'s dignity?
This is what it meant:

at the roll call,
some anchoring wish —

or a shared shoe,
a black rouge of rationed

coffee in the camp,
to dodge selection for the flames...

Truth to tell:
there's barely been a day

when the filth of the barracks,
the fury of the camps

didn't obsess my heart;
But I will go with you to Birkenau,

near the slain beasts
of the old crematoriums,

where everywhere you walk,
you are walking on human ash.

I want to leave something
sturdy in this world,

maybe a book
of live-to-tell truth,

grace and vitamins,
for those to come.

More than anything, son,
what I've wanted to tell you:

there was a woman of courage
in the camp,

and she shepherded me,
kindled me to keep me alive.

A clear light seemed to shore her
(as if we were seeing

a one-woman sunrise,
an unstoppable human dawn),

so that she garnered strength to share
her meager scraps,

strength to carry the ones
still minus an alphabet,

making up soothing rhymes,
little puddles of sound...

Like so many,
she died of typhus.

And after liberation,
in the DP camp,

amid the chaos, I prayed
my children would inherit

a portion of her spirit.
And it's true,

you have some of her fearlessness,
her passion, you do.

Son, why didn't I see it before?
How my hardscrabble prayer,

in its dove's arc,
was answered.

THE SINGING FOREST

A red and ocher forest near Žilina
was my earliest classroom,

my first wondrous library
and lavish sanctuary:

on autumn hillsides,
my just-widowed mother and I

would cull plump woodberries
and wild mushrooms.

As a towheaded, willing boy,
I was taught to venerate

each forest thing,
singing in Slovak,

in the treble clef,
dobre, dobre

(good, good)
as my spellbound eyes passed

from branch to glistening branch.
Don't stray too far, son;

*don't step on the wand
of the* Vila,

the sweet-souled forest witch,
my mother would tease me —

So when the schnapps-fueled German soldier
gestured and said,

Do you hear that music?
That's the singing forest,

I was whisked, rabbit quick,
to my childhood copse

to Mother's robust rendition
of *How Does the Czar Drink His Tea?*

to the stone ribs
of the flying castle of Lietava —

Amid the crows'
tattooing caws, I detected

a strange bellowing,
then I glimpsed them

above the Nazi's spittle-bright
jest and helmet:

a row of men hooked
to dispiriting poles.

And suddenly I grasped:
my cry, my unchecked agony

would be subsumed by theirs —
Dangling, ebbing, I imagined

Mother's consoling alto:
Quick, Slavomir, focus

on the streak of the deer,
like an August star —

Then, in a moment's match-burst,
someone cut me down,

convinced I was a corpse,
but I was stubbornly alive —

And the immense light, the prevailing
singing that supplants crucifixion,

parted the forest.

I. A Girl of Vichy France

Blue paper filled her first windows,
not snatch-gossip sparrows

or the sun's reveille
but a verdict of iron;

perfect-for-hopscotch parks,
Seine-lit stores

with exquisite engines
of this-and-not-that

became, for "me-first" Sabine, impossible:
everywhere almond-green greatcoats

and boots like trampling hooves—
Bells of invaded parishes

tolled the sallow hours;
fine-made mezuzahs were mauled

by braying patriots,
and learners whose hair

would never thin or silver
were banished from their desks and inkwells:

École du Garçons, rue Neuve Saint-Pierre,
École des Filles, rue de L'ave Maria...

Where a cellophane France,
all fly-apart assurances,

renounced Sabine and her peers —
plane trees and regretful plaques

urging *N'oubliez pas*
or *Ne les oublion jamais,*

so that the questing pilgrim
or the alert passerby

might perceive,
in the midst of the sumptuous city,

soulhollows
where even the smallest Parisians

were obliterated without pity.

ii. A Resemblance

A contrite Paris has unveiled
photos and still-vile documents to decry

the specter of sundering trains
aiming star-patched children

through tunnels and laconic fields:
11,400 hopes —

Sabine, who was hidden in the mountains,
has nudged me to city hall

to live awhile in the duress,
the dog's-snarl cosmos

of never-grown deportees.
But will Parisians take time,

Sabine laments, to bear in mind
the children of verboten sidewalks,

verboten parks?
Look, Sabine remarks,

before his transport to Poland,
a brave boy left on a wall,

We are leaving Drancy in good spirits,
but for the traveler, the commuter,

today Drancy, where we Jews were held,
is only a place you whisk by

on the train to the airport—
Near us, some vying kids

are unsettled
by the uncanny resemblance

between a child in a yellowed photo
and a schoolgirl who lingers,

crestfallen, hollow before
the image of her deported twin —

When the welter of kids passes,
Sabine whispers:

Ma pauvre petite!
Hurry, we've got to help her:

she was too stunned to notice
the girl in the picture lived!

III. Ghosts

Sabine with her forest-colored blouse
fills my summer rooms

on the rue des Rosiers;
on Sabbath mornings,

Hebrew singing floats
from the temple on the rue Pavée,

competing with the voluble
pigeons who adore my ledge.

Clear-eyed Sabine is quick to notice
how my writing desk faces

the École du Travail with its doleful plaque
blessing deported pupils and teachers —

So the war has become
your *devoirs:*

Yes, Sabine, my homework
that I can't seem to escape:

My friend, when I entered your flat,
I could feel it in my bones:

the family that once lived here
was deported!

No surprise in your neighborhood:
the Pletzl!

Sabine, yesterday my landlord read
my poem rooted in the war

and revealed: as a small girl,
she was hidden like you.

Poet, from cellar to cellar, I remember
I held onto, of all things,

a picture book about a magical goat,
inscribed by my witty father:

This storybook belongs
to Mademoiselle Sabine

the way Paris once belonged
to Marie Antoinette —

Somehow having that book
helped me to endure

the cold and fear —
And when I returned to Paris,

it was to a world of ghosts,
the void shaped

by my murdered generation.
Was it the same for you

in the epidemic —
when you returned,

after so many deaths,
to San Francisco?

Do the men, like my school friends,
still come to you in dreams?

At the exhibit, I thought:
Small as they were in life,

my playmates,
their souls must be immense by now.

THE FIT

1. Loïc's Caveat

Warning: this takes place far from the Paris
of pert crocuses and foie gras,

of clerk-blessed leeks tucked
in a market basket

for a valentine's soup.
Perhaps this is a Paris,

jeune homme, a France
you'd prefer not to know?

II. A Lover's Invocation

In his rooms rife with textiles and bibelot,
where I will never be middle-aged C —

but *jeune homme,*
old Loïc invokes his first love:

Luc — impossibly black lashes
against tallow-pale skin —

berry black or cloak black —
a lucent beauty deemed

useless, irrelevant in the laager,
an Orphic beauty that was later

savaged by dogs.

III. **Ashes and Peonies**

The immodest spring Loïc imparted
his gripping past,

an April and May
of attention-must-be-paid

pink and ivory peonies,
I lived for the first time in Paris —

near the poignant, starkly sculpted
memorial to the deportees.

Impossible to cross
the bridge to Ile Saint-Louis, the Marais,

without recalling
pink triangles and shaming stars,

so that the war's pervading ash
was subtly woven

into the skein of even my sunniest,
river-blessed days,

as if by some unflagging harbinger, some
night-beaked, insistent bird.

IV. **Youth**

Jeune homme, listen, in those days, we had
the Zazou style:

snappy clothes,
and longish, layered hair that cost

a bundle for upkeep.
I met my first love, Luc,

on the esplanade,
with my bold, impetuous

band of Zazous.
But Luc wasn't a Zazou;

he had no detectable style,
no affectations;

he was genial, quick-witted,
rather small like me,

and lightly freckled,
with those long, impressive lashes —

And when I listen to Loïc,
I think:

How two boys ignite,
fit together,

is a burst of summer fireworks,
a radiant cartwheel —

Embracing in scouted-out basements
and fusty attics,

or emboldened between
burly rolls of cloth

in Luc's meticulous father's shop —
they were purblind,

a worldlier Loïc explains,
and, in their youth, believed

risible Hitler would never
enter Alsace;

high-hearted Jew and Gentile,
they were purblind and thought

their love, their passion,
made all routes possible.

v. Loïc in Disguise

A clock in an Alsatian square
adjusted at pistol-point

to Berlin time —
What do you want,

guns or butter,
the broadcast Führer bellowed;

Guns! Guns! —
and a shamefaced Loïc witnessed

Antoine the Jewish shopkeeper
bullied and pummeled to clean

paving stones with a reluctant tongue,
urbane, imperious Antoine,

who was never seen again...
Then lacerating news:

the Gestapo had arrested Luc.
Marius, Loïc's savvy neighbor,

counseled Loïc in secret:
My son is your size.

He's got a Hitler uniform;
I'm sure it would fit.

Put it on, Loïc,
and get your Luc out.

But when Loïc reached him,
Luc declared: *No, I can't come with you.*

If I leave my ailing father,
I'll never be free.

VI. The Red "Confession"

Cornered by the police,
in a brute-fisted time

when ill will and innuendo
bloomed into evidence,

hectored to denounce
the other "inverts" of Mulhouse,

Loïc was battered
for ten days, ten nights,

the word *Schweinehund* hurled
on swift, sullying

comets of spit,
till at last he gave the Gestapo,

with their force majeure,
what they demanded:

his signature.
But the unstanched blood

from his maimed hands made
his long-in-coming "confession"

illegible...

VII. Cosmos of Silence

The decades of silence, fetid silence,
have to do

with six leaden months in the laager
at Schirmeck

in the chilly valley of the Bruhre,
have to do

with six months of tip trucks, rock quarries,
meager rutabaga soup,

have to do
with rampant vermin, mysterious injections,

and braggart terror — swaggering terror —
cutting its wide swath

through the numbing camp.
One of the youngest internees,

Loïc too easily became
terror's pawn, terror's

obedient ghost,
an unprotesting ghost —

as at pitiless roll call,
when another young man,

condemned to execution,
was spurred and kicked

to the glum center of the square
that the unnerved prisoners formed.

Stricken, resistless, unable
to cry out, Loïc recognized

his lost, candle-pale love.
Then, before the cowed, assembled camp,

the SS stripped Luc
naked, shoved over his irreplaceable

freckled head
an impervious pail

(debasing tin that distorted,
amplified his shrieks),

and, while classical music blared,
they unleashed,

they unleashed —

VIII. **The Recurring Roll Call**

For years, festering years,
that roll call has replayed,

left me howling
in the middle of the night.

Please, when will I stop
having to dream this, tell this?

Hundreds of prisoners were made
menaced spectators

to Luc's monstrous end—
Where are they?

Why do they remain silent?

IX. **The Fit**

The eureka of Luc's bold pebble
at the casement.

Two breakneck bicycles.
Then hours in the solace

of the bliss-conferring forest:
in the moon-dappled copse,

a white, inquisitive owl, a hand
over Loïc's mouth to hush

their giddy coupling.
Under the silvery,

breeze-stirred leaves,
how two boys fit together

is a buoyant dream
of breath, communion, trust —

With detectable pride,
Loïc, in his dapper scarf, pets

the blue Gascon hounds he breeds
to counter the impinging

terror of dogs
engendered by Luc's

spectacular murder;
his fussy-fingered tenderness,

his gnarled, prevailing hands
on their sun-flecked fur

is the present's triumph.
And as he revels

in his entrusted animals,
a skillful tailor,

Loïc contemplates
that once-upon-a-time,

ecstatic fit, praising
one imperishable face —

the startling lashes,
berry black or cloak black...

MY SECRET THRONE

Solomon Perel

Pliant, openhanded,
that's how the river appears

when I reach it,
though in recurrent dreams

it raged, stern
as the relentless Styx —

The insouciant moon that was,
at the war's onset,

a timid moth
trapped in the river's flux

rises and blanches
the teal, cool banks,

and suddenly
the four Aprils of *Tell No One,*

the marathon Mays
of *Hide Your Circumcision*

(the long months
of my impossible gambit,

a bar-mitzvah boy
concealed for years

as a staunch Hitler Youth)
begin to sail out of sight...

Summoned to the blighted arena
of *beforehand,*

the embittering river
where my adored brother and I

were bullied apart,
I begin a dialogue

with the winter-haired revenant
who rises in the water's mirror,

singing in unstinting Hebrew,
How sweet it is to sit

surrounded by your brothers,
for now I envision

my tenacious brothers,
David and Isaak,

and the blessed ghosts
of so many camp-banished friends

here in unison
at the river's hem,

a bolstering chorus —
then, in a flash, wonder

if it might be possible to devise
an ad hoc ballad that begins:

I know you won't believe me, friends,
if I tell you I recall my bris,

graced by the rabbi's
far-seeing prayer:

Let this child live...
A dispelling breeze comes,

and Jupiter dots
the kohl-dark distance,

as if this reedy riverbank
where I wept at fourteen,

capsized,
in frantic exodus from Lodz,

could become at last
my secret throne,

and this quickening current
the abetting blue that ferried

Moses in his inviolable basket...

THE GALICIAN SPADE

As a barricaded teen,
in the war's brackish cauldron

of less than and more than, you buried
your wind-and-moon-blessed testimony —

With a way-showing map you've crafted
from unremitting memory,

near L'viv, I find the hoped-for,
ivy-laden wall, the upraised yew

of your immutable homeplace;
Father, I grip the unerring spade

to resurrect an adamant,
war-made seer who insisted

all the tears of his demeaned world
would flow into the heart of God.

THE RAVINE

"The Holocaust by Bullets," Ukraine, 1941–1944,
Nina Raufimovna Lisitsina

In my fifth
holy year on earth,

undeterred,
I climbed out of a corpse-filled,

breakspirit ravine,
clutching the roots of trees

(so beautiful,
the god-tall cypresses,

the grandfather pines
in that part of the Crimea),

and groped my way, gingerly,
toward my twilit village,

the lone, itinerant survivor.
The pull, the rose light

of home
is unkillable.

THREE KINGS

When my belittled village was eclipsed
by pillaging soldiers,

quick as a windblown kite,
my baking aunt coaxed me

into her privy's acrid underworld.
Banished from the flour-dusted

blossoms of her apron,
I was too green to beseech God

or beautiful Queen Esther.
Unmoored, I fastened on the bookish

name of my slingshot —
Aramis, Aramis, Aramis —

as if in that shit-drenched dark,
I could summon, abracadabra,

the slingshot's Y-shaped, trusty wood,
and from that musketeer mantra, I acquired

a little certainty, a little stamina, a little consolation,
like three resplendent kings

come to a filthy manger.

SALUTE

Dawn upon dawn,
my father's whereabouts

a fierce morsel in the mouth of a sphinx;
for sixty fogbound years,

not a word, and then
a key-cold message from Russia:

Father's remains
had been recovered and interred

in a resting place
for fallen Germans.

Month after abrading month,
my mother had mailed

a tin-kept sum to ensure
the burial of luckless

soldiers lost abroad,
then spurred me,

with her dying breath,
to solve the mystery.

Suffused with the titan birches' beauty,
dressed in overdue

atoms of grief—
my mother's persistent charity

miraculously repaid—
suddenly I witnessed,

past my father's terse marker,
two white unhampered horses

saunter from the haze-wrapped woods
and halt,

their riffled manes
as dazzling as epaulettes.

And after a bygone calm
that the breeze-swept stallions lowered

like an unbelievable drawbridge,
I clutched my shawl,

remembering Mother's elating
live-and-let-live laugh

as she claimed Father so favored
his saddle and ambling bay,

God must have given him
the soul of a centaur—

Then the pert allies
vanished into the haze,

the wind-tugged woods—
Dawn upon dawn,

and the hush after the kudos
of their trumpet-clear hooves:

Silence, the keenest salute.

THE YOUNG DOCTOR FROM KRAKOW

1. **The Brand**

My hands were taken from me long ago.
And in the downfall, the gust

of the invasion, my face
was the face of Rembrandt's

in-a-rush Polish Rider —
do you know that painting?

What wind-insistent Memory retrieves
from the arduous past's

dampened fire: I was an Adonis,
a dashing prodigy —

and my widowed mother pinned
all her outsized hopes

on my enviable looks,
on my healer's diligence.

As Tomek, a maudlin friend,
a cabaret hound

and deluded Nazi sympathizer,
once put it:

Our dear, handsome Tadeusz
is a far-from-worthless Pole,

who, with his hay-colored curls,
could pass for a highborn German…

And now, when I hear
some timeworn aunt or snow-haired

neighbor in a Krakow doorway
hail me as *Doctor,*

a calling I abandoned at the war's end —
the war that took, in a raucous blast,

my wife and school-bound daughter —
the title stings like a blunt reproach

and brands me
like implacable iodine.

II. **The Menagerie**

When the Germans came
for my agile hands,

the unabated Germans babbling
of "life unworthy of life,"

as a "requisitioned" Pole,
a novice in their menagerie,

initially I was shunted toward
yellowish-pink vials of phenol,

for what I later discerned
was the plebeian task

of quick, brute elimination,
but Marek from my university days

spoke up on my behalf:
No, no, Tadeusz has greater skills!

For a brief while,
my celebrated surgeon's hands

went haywire,
after I was bullied to inject

viruses into the bodies
of young "subjects."

Marek tried to steady me:
Tadeusz, remember, you're a scientist!

And beyond the grim syringes,
beyond Marek's tale of a Jewish girl

deliberately submerged in gelid water,
were the faces of my own children.

How could I go on, a party to
this plunder-is-commonplace world

as deadly as nightshade
or prussic acid, replete

with bestial "research"?
How could I close my being

to the pleas of children
foundering, enfeebled?

Doctor!

III. **Escape to Budapest**

What deplorable ghosts,
what coarse weaponry,

the camp made of my hands,
but with my sister Alka's help,

her tucked-away *marks* and *zlotys,*
I fled my "duties" at last.

Like the fleet, urgent Polish Rider,
I burned for a new destination.

I raced to Budapest, where I became,
to my utter disbelief,

a hero for a time,
having extracted a bullet

from a well-loved rabbi;
I basked in the shawl-like goodwill

of the grateful Jews of Pest.
After Auschwitz, it felt

so redeeming to be of use,
to render honorable work,

to see my patients vital again.
But what's the meaning of healing

if the rough-and-tumble world merely
annuls your work?

Where the dapper river of waltzes
darkened with blood—

red chord,
red chord

I begged this question
of my shut-mouthed God—

iv. **The Telling**

My hands were taken from me long ago
in battered Poland,

but in my old age,
as if in an annealing legend,

the gravity and beauty of my revered
Hippocratic oath,

my ransomed hands
are restored to me in part

by the immeasurable force,
the bonanza of my son Josef's

sea blue, fathoming gaze,
my unmarred son's

heart and recognition
of the errant science

I aided and endured
in the marathon of the laager.

Liberty: sixty years
in the telling,

and only now, with my steadying cane,
do I unkennel —

here they come! — the implacable
hounds of all that occurred?

PRIMO LEVI REMEMBERING DANTE
IN AUSCHWITZ

The havoc and shove of the contentious
camp kitchen

is a half mile away,
and with ramshackle poles

over our shoulders
to lift the hefty pot that holds

the day's lackluster ration,
in the laager we filch

a nearly unriled hour,
lush as a furlough,

thanks to Jean,
the commando's clerk —

quick as a cardsharp — who's devised
a sly detour.

After chilly hours of scouring
an underground tank,

the powdery, stolid rust burning
my lids and throat,

what a boon
to breathe the June air,

to feel,
even in the swastika's shadow,

the soul still
capable of so much —

The distant Carpathians appear,
to my puzzlement and delight,

cleaner, closer,
in late spring, the still-wintry cusp

pale and inviting as an opened
packet of schoolroom chalk —

Who knows why,
in the midst of the camp's

deranging chimneys,
stanzas of Dante's *Commedia*

mysteriously rise up
in my downcast being.

With all-out grit,
I combat bothersome gaps

in my recall of Dante's lines,
then recover Ulysses's rousing words

to his dispirited sailors:
For brutish ignorance

your mettle was not made;
you were made men,

to follow after knowledge and excellence.
And in shipwrecked Auschwitz,

we jeered ration-carriers vanish;
in the crow's nest fashioned by Dante's

time-eliminating music,
Jean and I are lifted,

riveted by the Greek warrior's
reckless bravura,

by arriving poetry — tireless
as save-the-day hooves,

unfailing as the taproot oath
of a milk brother...

JULIEK'S VIOLIN

Even here?
In this snowbound barrack?

Suddenly, the illicit sounds
of Beethoven's concerto

erupt from Juliek's smuggled violin,
suffusing this doomsday shed

teeming with the trampled
and the barely alive,

realm of frostbite and squalor,
clawing panic and suffocation —

Insane, God of Abraham,
insanely beautiful:

a boy insisting
winter cannot reign forever,

a boy conveying his brief,
bounded life

with a psalmist's or a cantor's
arrow-sure ecstasy —

One prison-striped friend
endures to record

the spellbinding strings,
the woebegone —

and the other,
the impossible Polish fiddler,

is motionless by morning,
his renegade instrument

mangled
under the haggard weight

of winter-killed, unraveling men.
Music at the brink of the grave,

eloquent in the pitch dark,
tell-true, indelible,

as never before,
as never after —

Abundance,
emending beauty,

linger in the listening,
truth-carrying soul of Elie,

soul become slalom swift,
camp shrewd, uncrushable;

abundance, be here, always here,
in this not-yet-shattered violin.

A GREAT BEAUTY

And when her son never returned
from the meant-to-crush-him camps,

the crucible of Poland,
always-hard-at-work Isa slept

for endless hours,
and once, under her lids, she was led,

by diligent female Virgils,
to a vast meadow

where an inspirited Isa embraced,
one by one,

countless women who remained
in mourning for their cherished sons.

Gallant and stricken,
together the myriad bereaved

but defiant women formed
an ever-widening circle,

prodigal with bitter tears,
and then, suddenly,

like a jackdaw darting
from eave to sun-drenched eave,

something flew between the throats
of the grieving,

heart-gutted mothers,
and a great beauty arose:

In the dream, Isa recalled,
the singing of the harrowed women

with war-taken sons
hushed the world's barrenness.

In the dream, the startling river of sound
altered the embattled earth.

THE POSTCARD OF SOPHIE SCHOLL

There is the lightning-white moment
when I learn —

the way my costive train to Krakow
stopped

and I woke to find myself,
in jostling twilight,

at the Auschwitz platform —
that the Italian postcard

I garnered in Milan years ago
as a genial talisman

isn't of a pipe-dreaming
Italian boy,

no, no, but an androgynous
image of Sophie Scholl,

the young, intrepid resistance heroine —
as if I'd registered,

in my Schubert-adoring daughter,
my school-resisting son,

a fire undetected before:
Doric-strong nouns demanding

*What would you undertake
to stop tyranny?* —

stouthearted nouns:
integrity, probity, courage;

in benighted Munich,
the spit-in-the-eye swiftness,

the unbossed bloom
of a crossed-out swastika,

the fierce integrity
in the gust of the word *freedom*

sprayed over the walls
and ramparts of a deranged

fatherland that rent flesh
as if it were foolscap —

Someday you will be
where I am now,

a steely, premonitory Sophie
proclaimed to the rapacious

Nazi tribunal that rushed her
to execution —

Gazer, collector, in clarity's name,
look close, then closer:

it's not just a bud-sweet,
pensive beauty,

a *bel ragazzo*'s charm;
all these years:

it's the spirit of crusading youth
that I've cherished.

THE CONFISCATED SHOES

As many barbarisms as stars —

In the dizzying room
at Auschwitz, behind terse glass:

here's a brown lotus,
and here, and here —

heart-stopping galaxy of leather,
raging, attesting:

the first noun that fire ravishes
is *freedom*.

AUSCHWITZ, ALL HALLOWS

Look, we have made
a counterpoint

of white chrysanthemums,
a dauntless path

of death-will-not-part-us petals
and revering light;

even here,
even here

before the once-wolfish ovens,
the desecrating wall

where you were shot,
the shrike-stern cells

where you were bruised
and emptied of your time-bound beauty—

you of the confiscated shoes
and swift-shorn hair,

you who left,
as sobering testament, the scuffed

luggage of utter hope
and harrowing deception.

Come back, teach us.
From these fearsome barracks

and inglorious fields
flecked with human ash,

in the russet-billowing hours
of All Hallows,

let the *pianissimo*
of your truest whispering

(vivid as the crunched frost
of a forced march)

become a slowly blossoming,
ever-voluble hearth

revealing to us
(the baffled, the irresolute,

the war torn, the living)
more of the fire

and attar of what it means
to be human.

NOTES

RIDERS ON THE BACK OF SILENCE

"A woman of light in the camps": I was thinking of Lili Gershon here.

Some portions of the sequence were inspired by events in the life of Daniel Mendelsohn, as detailed in his memoir *The Lost,* and in the life of my friend Harry Mattison, the photojournalist.

THE SINGING FOREST

"The singing forest" was a Nazi euphemism for a torture site that involved hangings.

SABINE WHO WAS HIDDEN IN THE MOUNTAINS

This poem is for Beatrice, Erika, and Ellen.

THE FIT

This semifictionalized poem is based primarily on the life of Pierre Seel, one of the very few survivors of Hitler's vicious edict against homosexuals who spoke publicly about his arrest and internment.

A section of the poem is based on the experience of Gad Beck (b. 1923), the author of *An Underground Life: Memoirs of a Gay Jew in Nazi Berlin.*

The slick-haired Zazous were jazz and bebop aficionados who rebelled by wearing big or garish clothing, similar to the zoot suit craze in America. In Vichy France, they were increasingly persecuted as the war went on.

MY SECRET THRONE

This poem is inspired by the final scene in Agnieszka Holland's great film *Europa Europa,* in which Solomon Perel, on whom the historical drama is based, sings in Hebrew by a river. In the poem, I imagine it as the Bug River in Poland where he was separated from his brother Isaak in 1939 during the Nazi invasion of Poland. The story of Perel, who was born in 1925 in Peine, near Brunswick, Germany, and who, after the war, emigrated to Israel, is a maze of heart-stopping escapes and "miracles," including successfully passing himself off a Hitler Youth for four years in an academy dangerously close to his hometown of Peine — a quick-witted, improbable odyssey he kept secret for years.

THE RAVINE

The poem is based on the testimony of survivor Nina Roufimovna Lisitsina.

SALUTE

This poem is based on events in the life of Renate Pesch. Her sons, Achim Kramer and Thomas Pesch, aided me with this poem.

THE YOUNG DOCTOR FROM KRAKOW

This sequence is rooted in passages of Robert Jay Lifton's exhaustive and fearless book *The Nazi Doctors*.

PRIMO LEVI REMEMBERING DANTE IN AUSCHWITZ

Peter Balakian's essay "Poetry in Hell" inspired a rereading of Primo Levi's indispensable memoir *Survival in Auschwitz*.

JULIEK'S VIOLIN

This poem was inspired by a passage in Nobel Laureate Elie Wiesel's *Night* and is dedicated, with deepest respect, to Elie Wiesel.

A GREAT BEAUTY

This poem was sparked by visits to the Käthe Kollwitz museums in Berlin and Cologne, and also by Henryk Gorecki's Third Symphony, with its emphasis on motherhood and mourning. This poem is dedicated to poet Ellen Hinsey, who encouraged my interest in Kollwitz.

THE POSTCARD OF SOPHIE SCHOLL

Sophie Scholl (1921–1943) became an international symbol of resistance when she was swiftly executed, along with her brother, Hans, and their friend, Christoph Probst, for distributing anti-Nazi leaflets at Munich University and for their part in the White Rose resistance movement.

The artwork referred to in the poem is a lithograph by Bruno Bruni.

Hans Scholl crossed out swastikas on the walls of Munich. After his death, a note was found on his desk, a quote from Stefan George: "Cross, for a long time you will remain the light of this earth."

ABOUT THE AUTHOR

Cyrus Cassells's poetry has garnered a Lannan Literary Award, a Lambda Literary Award, the William Carlos Williams Award, a Pushcart Prize, two NEA grants, and best-of-the-year citations from *Publishers Weekly* and *Library Journal*. *Still Life with Children: Selected Poems of Francesc Parcerisas* and *My Gingerbread Shakespeare*, his first work of fiction, are forthcoming. A professor of English at Texas State University–San Marcos, he divides his time between Austin, Santa Fe, and Paris, and works on occasion in Barcelona as a translator of Catalan poetry.

Since 1972, Copper Canyon Press has fostered the work of emerging, established, and world-renowned poets for an expanding audience. The Press thrives with the generous patronage of readers, writers, booksellers, librarians, teachers, students, and funders — everyone who shares the belief that poetry is vital to language and living.

MAJOR SUPPORT HAS BEEN PROVIDED BY:

The Paul G. Allen Family Foundation

Amazon.com

Anonymous

Arcadia Fund

Diana and Jay Broze

Beroz Ferrell & The Point, LLC

Mimi Gardner Gates

Golden Lasso, LLC

Gull Industries, Inc.
on behalf of William and Ruth True

Carolyn and Robert Hedin

Lannan Foundation

Rhoady and Jeanne Marie Lee

National Endowment for the Arts

New Mexico Community Foundation

Penny and Jerry Peabody

Joseph C. Roberts

Cynthia Lovelace Sears and Frank Buxton

Washington State Arts Commission

Charles and Barbara Wright

To learn more about underwriting Copper Canyon Press titles,
please call 360-385-4925 ext. 103

The Chinese character for poetry is made up of two parts: "word" and "temple." It also serves as pressmark for Copper Canyon Press.

The interior text is set in Baskerville 10, a digital reworking by František Štorm of the eighteenth-century English types of John Baskerville. Book design and composition by Valerie Brewster, Scribe Typography. Printed on archival-quality paper.